Angola, America

'But prisons do not disappear problems, they disappear human beings.'
~ Angela Davis

'To converse is to risk the performance of what's held by the silence.'
~ Claudia Rankine

Angola, America

Sammy Weaver

Winner of the
Mslexia Poetry Pamphlet
Competition

Seren is the book imprint of
Poetry Wales Press Ltd.
Suite 6, 4 Derwen Road, Bridgend, Wales, CF31 1LH
www.serenbooks.com
facebook.com/SerenBooks
twitter@SerenBooks

The right of Sammy Weaver to be identified as
the author of this work has been asserted in accordance
with the Copyright, Designs and Patents Act, 1988.

© Sammy Weaver, 2022

ISBN: 978-1-78172-700-3

A CIP record for this title is available from the British Library.

The publisher acknowledges the financial assistance of the Books Council of Wales.

Cover artwork: Zigmunds Lapsa

Printed in Bembo by 4Edge, Hockley

Contents

[origin story]

with a flint blade / he incised
a dozen cruciforms in his own torso /

smudged into each cut
a pigment of charcoal and soot /

almandine and quartz
to ensure each cross glistened /

epidermis long-rotted / what is left is this
map in the connective tissue

of the pain and losses / a scripture
unchanged through millennia

of change /   still / down the backstreets
of baton rouge / boys sit in rows /

under their eyes / the stitch and whine
of guns etching droplets / in ink

[correspondence : letter]

Do you remember the first letter you sent
addressed *Dear stranger / friend*?
The first thing I noticed was the loops
& hooks of your handwriting, each *i*
dotted with a little moon. Each word flattening
at its base as if like my grandmother you held
a ruler as you wrote to keep the lines from drifting
off the page. Under your name: *DR 561438*
& the first thing you asked: *why wish to make a friend*
of a man on death row? The first letter I sent
never reached you, perhaps it is still soaring above
the blue bars of Mother Atlantic or perhaps it is lost
in the prison's postroom or got tossed in the trash —
my words leaching in the Louisiana rain.

[body, flooded]

Existing as myth: the Mississippi
missing her sister, the sea, so badly
flooded the penitentiary. Or the fact
of water like this? She breached the
boundaries of her levees because her body
is one of effluvium & freedom, seeking
the easiest possible route downhill to complete
herself. Because inmates shifted sandbags
to keep themselves within their cells.
Because they became purveyors of silt,
which is to witness what kind of self settles
when left behind. Would you rather twist
in eddies towards the gulf, which is a mouth,
or live with just enough air to keep you alive?

[body, blue]

your brother on death row is learning to blow
his breath into the mouth of a manikin
the ongoing bellows of his lungs gifting
life into its artificial windpipe his palms
enact the non-existent heart by pressing
onto its rubber chest as if your brother
could resuscitate this lifelike dummy that will
never know what it is to like to live nor live to die
meanwhile the valves of your brother's heart
open & close like a series of trapdoors
meanwhile leaves somewhere are composing
oxygen from his carbon dioxide meanwhile
imprisoned brothers are held together
by chlorophyll & its preference for blue light

[correspondence : another year]

the grey static of the dashboard ignites into a ringtone
        ignites into a woman's voice pale-polite

as a white picket fence in the still of morning:
        hello, this is a free call from _____

an incarcerated individual at louisiana state penitentiary,
        this call is not private & may be monitored,

you may start the conversation now
        & the line ignites into song as you sing to me

happy birthday & because birth is death in reverse
        i imagine blowing a candle out backwards, sucking

the orange talons into the prison of my lungs,
        the wax congealing up the wick, the match lying

down in its box, the rush of our bodies diminishing
        inside the bodies of our mothers

[measure]

if the body is a body of water
you say I am an upland reservoir in yorkshire —
standing still at depth the height of a hill,
saying nothing of my drowned museum of farms
& steeples, saying nothing of my pre-industrial
slender-eel-of-a-river-beginning, lake of flooded
restraint, tank of measure & amnesia

if the body is a body of water
i say you are a bayou in low-lying acadiana —
lianas climbing to the sky climb down to earth,
your litany of wading ibises, spindles of their legs
steeped in the reflected stars, your abundance
of crawfish & spanish moss, your life brackish
& drained by state, reversing its course every day

[history of insignia / missing black bear, state animal of louisiana]

begin with my mother twisting her face
        into a ball of whiteness, saying she prefers

to remain neutral. i say, neutral like milk,
        state beverage of louisiana, pale tincture

welling in the temple of the breasts, baby mammalian elixir.
        i say neutral like white perch, state fish of louisiana,

also known as fisherman's pest as they prey on
        baitfish & other fishes' eggs. i say neutral like magnolia,

state flower of louisiana, tender flesh of petals
        packed in like swan's feathers. i say neutral like oyster shell,

state gemstone of louisiana, its ripples of silver light.
        i say neutral like sugarcane jelly, state jelly of louisiana,

acres of plantation simmering down into this
        off-yellow slice of it wobbling on our plates

[state soap]

Best applied under cold to tepid water
because the state will not grant hot.
Because this soap-block in the shower-block
in the DR-block at the back of all other blocks

was never meant to lather. Who thought to extract
the fat from an alligator only to neutralise
its wretched scent? Hold in your palms
the colour of hospital gowns, a shade of bile.

Is it free, which is to say, is it a gift
if it rids the skin of softness? This soap-bar
is not a metaphor for the state of corrections
attempting to cleanse the bodies of inmates

undressed as slaves, again. Better then to leave
the beads of sweet sweat uncorrected.

[skin song]

Suppose the skin resists by shedding
every six weeks: oblivious, you slough off
the old self, the tiny petals of dead cells
confetti on the floor of your cell.
Suppose under a microscope the structure
of skin resembles a wall of bricks,
the surface layers burnt paper, curled
& crimped. Suppose the skin is a listener
with its millions of ribbony nerves & vessels
& the see-sawing mechanism of each hair
keeping the body from what it is not, inside
from outer & other. Suppose upon scrubbing
in the shower, flakes of you sluice down
the drain's municipal throat, becoming elsewhere.

[whiteness : beast mode]

'Because white men can't police their imagination black men are dying.'
~ Claudia Rankine

unbeknownst to him
& blind to themselves
boxy-visions of their eye-minds
as a puma or puma-human
of his hips
raising his whip in the liquid-like-air
akin to kin

walking to purchase bread & milk
the mist-spinning
have chosen him
slinking in the blades
or the mirage of a scorpion
an alien a demon
made scapegrace

now they have him
a made-up puppet
to their anxiety
[which is mine]
defines us from them
critter of luck & magic
of their chambers

fashioned savage
unspecifically melanistic
& in their muted freedom
they say *the gift of reason*
& select a white rabbit
to test the efficacy
noses laced with almond bitterness

[half a wolf]

[in 2012, to save money, prison warden burl cain, replaced human guards with wolf-dogs to patrol louisiana state penitentiary]

when the warden decided on wolf-dogs
at the boundary fence   when he crossed

feral with pet   did he forget the untame
element will always outshy the tame

desire to chase inmates?   as they catch
scent of them   the silver nebulas of their faces

turn   only wanting to flee from them
as their hackles yearn   only wanting the shelter

of the stars   which for now   are barbed wires
when the wolf in the half of them that is dog

recalls the dog in the half of them that is wolf
are they as full as moon?   O can any of this

elucidate why a domestic horse is
broken in   whilst a wild one is unbroken?

[search]

In the beginning the guard's gloved hands
pat you down, searching for weapons,
his touch is weaponized, the muted duty
of his movements smooth along each of your arms.
Soon the guard's touch is the only touch
from another
                        and you think of your mother
after bath time, the harbour of her chest
against yours, the rough-love of her towelling
you dry, reaching into all the nooks
and crannies, *no cabbages behind the ears*
she says. And yes, I guess searching the body
is another way of saying the body is a trove
of treasure and your touch a torch.

[ode to handcuffs]

handcuffs / you-as-love / are the hardest
to imagine / although a straitjacket might

admire your minimalism / love composed
of two holes / of two stainless steel halos /

when you've no one you are a hollow icon
/ longing to close around the rivulets

of wrists / O obtuse lover you draw
the palms together like prayer / O mother

of thumbcuffs / cousin of hogtie / your form
could be confused with an hourglass

/ or a celestial phenomenon /
the beginnings of a lunar eclipse / perhaps /

hidden within your love is a thin ratchet /
spine of angled teeth click click rattling

[anti-ode to angola rodeo]

[open to the public, angola prison rodeo is the longest-running prison rodeo in the US, inmates taking the most risks win cash]

Men dressed as miniature zebras bolt from
their cages into the dust bowl of the prison
coliseum, into the ritual of cowboy & steer.
Thunder of whoop & cheer as three lifers
herd together, throwing their ropes into the air
to lasso the bodied tornado of a bull, muscles
of shoulders swelling as water brought to a
rolling boil. One lifer clings onto a bronco, kicks in
the rowels of his spurs making the horse buck
& toss him like a tiddlywink to the mud. The guts
& glory of convict poker, to pluck a chip from between
the horns of a charging bull for to be gored
is to be both honour & disgrace, to be both man
& beast, broken-boned & returned to their cages.

[   ]

without knowing it   my whiteness permits
my witnessing   at relative distance

lets me send   a postcard from a holiday
a ledge   of privelege   is an edge

in which the risk of falling
                    from self is briefly felt

peer over to see an-
                    other in the *afterlife of slavery*

in the beforedeath of nowhistory
     the *narrative in an overexposed photo*

                              is difficult
to read as whiteness everpresses its silences

what else do I hold from myself? what must it take to cure this cult-
                              ure of lacuna?

[angola / museum]

because muse is inside museum & word
within world. because the origin, *mouseion,*
is greek via latin meaning *'seat of Muses',*

we see nine goddesses presiding over the arts
& sciences, their pale grimaces drifting over
the prison's exhibits. perusers of little songs

beckon us to gaze at the curios of felony
until we become absorbed in the wrong form
of thought-forms & lose our tongues.

because we have been known to itemise
persons into items. or yet again,
from latin, *musum* meaning *'muzzle'*

a mouth-shaped trap of straps & wires
made to restrain biting & raptures

[exhibit : electric chair]

You toured the parishes like a one-sided library,
not lending books, which are the minds of ghosts,
but collecting them. You toured the parishes
like a bus in reverse, judges dressed as conductors
returned passengers to where they came from
before birth. You toured the parishes like a medicine
man who administers with his rickety sticktool hands
poison mixed according to race-based reason. Hidden
within your masterpiece of terror the strength of mortise
& tenon. The voices of far-flung sons who said 'hello'
in suspicious tones. Of backwater daughters who
understood too soon. Of boondocks & brothers,
french quarters & lovers, all perishing under felony
which is just another word for lonely, or colony.

[exhibit : shiv]

I am all that exists
        of my maker's mind —

toothbrush whittled
        into a makeshift

knife — effigy of
        edges — mini-

javelin — I live by
        dominions of

skin — I slit —
        — & sink in

— to make victims
        of victims

which is what binds
        what splits them —

[exhibit : electric chair]

She still holds the grain of the tree
that made her. And the name they gave her,
Gruesome Gertie, sitting there in the museum
like a chair sits unassumingly except
she is rigged with leather at the legs
& wrists. Which southern tree was she?
A swamp cypress with her root buttress
submerged in the slow mirror of the bayou?
Back when her phloem flowed with sap
Back when she spoke only pollen & cymbals
of leaves to the wind. Now her oval knots
have blinked open the varnish as if all the tension
of living were translated in lignin. As if her manydead
left her like the memory of empty nests —

[death row hex]

let the lords of big pharma
& potassium
trinkets of air
blunt into a stub
of skin finding hindrance
of every vein buckle
reaches the stubborn muscle
let the chair reject its add-ons
& if it decides to keep them
short circuit from too much rain
of screeching wheels
let the mississippi hugging the prison
let the sun in the yard
let there be a bus

dam up the rivers of paralytic
so the glass vials become
let the nib of the needle
& scud across the surface
if all else fails let every wall
& blow before the venom
of your heart
of anodes & wires
let the electric grid
let the gurney with its refrain
return to our chapels of care
peel back to reveal the fat lip of mud
beat harder than any past
waiting to carry you home

[brood x]

The sky above his cell is full of cicadas.
Risen from their seventeen-year bunkers.
Resurrected from the darkness where they sucked
the tree-root syrup, growing into fat larvae.

He cannot see them trying out their new bodies,
their abdomens of ebony, the engine
of their filigree wings. He cannot hear
the hell-bent throttle of their song, each one
singing above the swarm. They fly beyond

the boundary fence where the guards
with guns. They fly beyond the bend
in the Mississippi river. All the while

he sits on his mattress, book in palm,
reading the sentence over and over again.

[escapism]

is what matters the matterless
space between the bars? — a freeway

for motes to drift back & forth —
the moon enters — unfolding her orb

into an oblong on the floor —
also — an octopus — versed in escapism —

drifts back & forth — in the hallway
coiling up her boneless body

of mantle & tentacles — she slips through
the porous boundary —

a pipistrelle echolocating the holes
in the steel dips & dives from cell to cell —

— most of all — quarks — those subatomic
particles whizzing through the solid walls

[nest / fence]

our father, from heaven looking down
the maximum security complex looks like
a cluster of chunky crosses, a flock of cherubs
spatchcocked on the surface of the earth
& grilled white by the sun. our father,
from earth looking up the maximum security
complex looks like heaven folded its airy
dancefloor into a blue box to be bored under.
well then! god bless the godless, the mother
duck with her congregation of ducklings
toddles in seeking asylum in the prison's
catless society. a nameless bird makes her nest
high in the barbed fence, crowning the boundary
of sin with twigs, feathers, pale-blue eggs

[asylum]

Dr. John, with his throat of rusty iron, got locked
in you, sang a sang for you, a seventeen-minute
anthem, driven by the beat of collapsing chains.
Kevin Gates, with a tear on his face, got locked
in you, sang a song for you, the tear remained
unchanged. Lil' Boosie, with his red eyes rolling
back inside his head, got locked in you, sang a
song for you, *they say I'm a role model but I ain't
got no role model*. Lead Belly, with the asylum of
his accordion & howl, got locked in you, sang
a song for you of how the boll weevil looked for
a home in the holes of the cotton. James Booker
got locked in you, sang a song for you, his fingers
singed the keys of the piano like flames in dry grass.

[terraforming a prison cell]

because whitey is still on the moon too
soon & elon musk on mars, she terraforms
this cell on earth to resemble earth.
she scatters lichen on the floors & walls,
their acid tongues rend the cement into soil
to allow the web of mycelium below
the thought of fruiting bodies, of blooming spores.
into the toxic atmosphere she introduces
a poultice of song & maybe in the soil
a pond. she angle grinds the iron bars, those cold
angels of angola, annealing them in a crucible
to produce a palm-sized bowl & compass.
she terraforms until only the dew is penitential
& the garden toad content to brood in it like a stone

[correspondence : videogram]

You sit in your cell watching on repeat
the thirty-second slice of setting sun

I sent. Through the small screen
of your tablet the sky reaches you

pixelated — juddery squares
of pink & orange.

You press play again
because your sun arcs below

the horizon of your barred window.
Because there is nothing

more lonely than a window,
except the drawing of a window

on a windowless wall. You lie back,
letting this relic of sunset flood your cell.

Notes

'[   ]' references Saidiya Hartman's term the 'afterlife of slavery' in *Lose Your Mother: A Journey Along the Atlantic Slave Route.* Claudia Rankine examines whiteness as an overexposed photo in *Just Us: An American Conversation.*

'[asylum]' references Lil' Boosie's lyrics in 'Mind of a Maniac'.

'[terraforming a prison cell]' references Gil Scott-Heron's lyrics in 'Whitey on the Moon' & Derek N. Otsuji's poem 'How to Garden'.

Acknowledgements

Thanks to Rishi Dastidar for his words of encouragement and for shortlisting some of these poems for the Nine Arches Press Primers 6 Scheme. Thanks to the editors at Nine Arches Press for publishing '[body, flooded]'.

Many thanks to Liz Berry, Fiona Benson and the bright minds on the Arvon course at Totleigh Barton for their encouragement and guidance.

Thanks to the MMU online workshop — Katie, Day, and Peter — who gave feedback on early drafts.

Many thanks to Lifelines, the UK-based charity that supports and befriends prisoners on Death Row throughout the United States, through letter writing.

Thank you, Bell, for the friendship and light.

Many thanks to Amy Wack from Seren and Debbie Taylor from Mslexia for giving these poems a brilliant home.

Eternal thanks to David, Osita and Maceo for knowing when words won't do.